Postmark Atlantis

By Paul Kareem Tayyar

Rhea,

Take a look at "1:33 am"
it was inspired by your poems.

Your Friend,

Level 4 Press, Inc.
ISBN: 978-1-933769-49-3

Dedication

For LeeAnne

Acknowledgements

Some Poems In This Collection First Appeared in the Following Magazines:

Bellowing Ark
Black Book Press
The Chaffin Journal
Pegasus
Ship of Fools
The Storyteller
Waterways
Write On

Preface

Born in a city no one remembers
Your back crippled in a war that was never declared

Tell us of orchids that grew into wreaths
On the doors of the wind
Tell us of children who jumped rope on an island of glass

Script your heritage into a poem you can carry
Inside the pockets of grace you smuggled when you escaped

Postmark Atlantis

Survivors

And that underground mural,
Ghosted like a labyrinth of clouds,
Our bodies tethered to a darkness that holds the voices
Of the painted like a
Thousand silent hostages,
Eyes closed to face a God
They are not certain
Anymore exists.

This is what it means to live:
Surrounded by a wound so vast
No amount of time could provide
Its healing,
We still insist on speaking in the hours while awake,
On dreaming in the hours when asleep.

Body Art

The fabric of the clouds looks like a braided tattoo,
And I wonder if the sky is like you, old man,
Who decades earlier,
In a moment of brashness,
Of whiskey-inspired sentimentality,
Carved the name of your girl onto your biceps on a night
You were certain your hard-luck ways
Were a thing of the past.

Is that what the wind is for you?
A cosmic sander, relentlessly trying to erase the poetry of a
Love you lost long ago?

1968

You can see the dove take shape in the form of a cloud
You can see how the cloud loses itself
With the arrival of winter

Watch how she shivers in the first wind from the east
Her wings trembling
Her eyes uncertain about which way is south

Everything she has ever known has been lost
With the ghost of the sun
She can do nothing but sing
While I stand helpless on the road below

The First of May

You see the horizon like a gypsy
Would: an easy mark, with pockets
Deep enough to pick without him
Having noticed.

You do not stop to eat until you
Are well into another landscape,
A clearing where the white river
That you forded sleeps like a
Child among the banks.

Last Night on the Telephone

Your father says the soil in Shiraz gives birth
To the most beautiful flowers,
He says that you could throw tennis balls into the dirt
And clovers would appear three days later,
Green petals attracting curious bees,
Producing lime-colored honey
That would slide down your throat
Like a river under the influence of heavy narcotics.

Someday you will see for yourself, he tells you,
Someday you will walk through these orchards
And see what I mean.

Young Man

Take the herbs from the kitchen
That you are certain to need
Take the flowers from the garden that you planted yourself

In time you will come to a place where the hour is ready
For the world you can make
From the things you have carried

Huntington Town

The pier like a sniper aiming at the moon
While the fishermen are lulled to sleep on their feet
By the sound of the waves

Oh penniless girl who walks among them speaking of God
Don't you know there are no sinners here among them?

They are dreaming of catfish and home
They talk in their slumbers of birthdays and wives

Farther on the all-night diner
That feeds the midnight surfers
The Kansas tourists
The pregnant teens and their rude-boy lovers
All stare out of the windows and onto the sea
They listen to jukebox tales of a world full of redemption

She speaks to herself of streets golden and long
But does not see she is standing upon one

Night

You looked just like Dionysus in the garden
Your hair was longer than mine had ever been

You took her by the hand and led her towards the river
You left her staring at the moon
You had vanished far beneath

The Last Dancer

Listen to the vinyl moon playing on the turntable of the sky,
Gramophone stars and the ballad of a beautiful world
That has lost its way.

You stand on the empty stage of this cabaret river,
You watch yourself in the mirrors above the bar
As you start to dance.

The Magician

You want so badly to tell how it's done
That you tell it to yourself each night before sleep,
Narrating a film that no one will see,
The sound of the rain like the beating of wings,
The applause you receive for keeping the secret.

Night Parable

A Prince who has declared war on the winds,
You sit cross-legged upon the face of the moon,
Fanned by comets, in conversation with boy soldiers
Who will become constellations,
You look down on your people,
And hope that the temples will hold
When the seasons change.

The girl with white eyelashes
Stalks the snows with her silence,
She does not have to look up to the sky to know
You are there, and that you are watching.

There will come a time, she is certain,
When all that you love will be lost,
The rivers will turn back on themselves in retreat,
The surface of the moon will crack beneath you
Like a frozen lake at first thaw,
Like a voice that has not spoken to someone in months.

For now,
The dreams that both of you have
Co-exist like a crossroads,
Two paths certain of more than the traveler
Who must make his decision,
A courtship where neither woman
Wants the hand that you offer.

Night Swimmer

You swim in the rain of our winter
Your muscles taut against the force of the wind

Though briefly you open your eyes
To see when the season will end
You close them again
To concentrate on the strength of your strokes
The disciplined breaths you must ration
To keep your body afloat through the storm

You know the ocean will protect all that you carry
And the dreams that you harbor
Will take care of themselves

This is why you swim only at night
Darkness a god
That provides a strength you could not have imagined

Bathers

In the river there was harvest,
You could see it rising from the depths
Like a mermaid coming up for air,
The hands of silent children
Plucking what they desired from the vines,
Leaving the rest to sing themselves to sleep
In the silence of beginning.

This was all you wanted,
To swim with gods inside a paradise you would not name,
Your bodies camouflaged by wheat and night,
Merging into fearless shapes,
A constellation with a thousand faces.

1:33am

It is the middle of the night.
You can hear the television from a neighboring apartment,
Inaudible dialogue like an arriving rain.
A car is pulling out of a driveway.
The wind that has been promised for days remains in exile,
A horse that refuses to leave its country stable,
Or a lover that pretends
Not to hear when her name is called.

When she gets up to turn on some music,
The bedroom lamp flickers for the briefest of moments,
Like someone whose sleep is threatened
By the sound of a door closing,
An intensive kiss she is not prepared to receive,
Before returning to the dreams
She was having before he arrived.

You should try to sleep yourself,
But this has become your favorite time of the day,
The speakers delivering the 1940s
From the second-floor apartment,
The scented warmth of the stove
That heats your midnight dinner,
The shadows falling across an empty room, space enough
For you to imagine her absence is only a matter of the hour,
And the darkness that it brings.

Sunday Morning Laughter

The bells of St. Catherine lead the faithful
From mass, the couples in dresses and suits
Holding hands as they pass, their children
Racing ahead to play in the grass—how you
Want their Sunday morning laughter to last!

The Mapmaker

You once skated on the lake of swans
And you spoke then of the future

You wondered if it would look like Albion
You wondered over which sea the sun would rise

For an hour you turned in careful circles
Carving bladed constellations into winter

You listened for the song of skies
You pretended not to notice when no song arrived

With your shoes left upon the shore
With your clothes lost to the shimmering winds

You noticed how the swans drew warmth
From their solitude
But parted ways on the lake at midnight

You watched your figure eights
Become more varied cartography
And followed your map into the country
You always hoped existed

Before

What is the palace of light but a sea with a ceiling
Arches where the paintings of gods distract us from waves

How many have missed the ride of their lives
Because they were too busy staring
At the waves earlier men had the courage to ride to the end

Father

He tucks the river into the breast of his pocket
Like a handkerchief,
And carries its song across the landscape of a world
He changes with his strength.

The children place their ears to his heart
And listen for the source of all creation,
They are carried into manhood by the current of his love.

Midsummer

Here among the graves
Your silence betrays you.

Call to him!

For he watches,
Like Oberon in the trees,
The rain his sorrow has delivered.

Paradise Blue

Language is the currency of another country
A place you left when you'd saved enough for the trip

The angels who gather your failures
Before they leave in the morning
Understand the concessions you made to be here at all

Rebirth

Trembling nudes, come in from the woods,
The muses you seek have left for the city.

Sit at the fire, wrap yourself in these blankets,
The food will be ready soon, your bed will be waiting.

Unfaithful

Your patience is a lie that you sustain
An ethos forged from the landscape of a second face

All the days that you are certain will be yours
Your brothers carry with them when they leave

Santa Barbara Go-Go Dancer

State Street midnight
College co-ed drinkers
Dreamers window-shopping
Vintage clothes and Jazz Age
Posters
Homeless striking yoga pose
Top-hat wearing *Vote for Gore*
Old seniors with their
Pearl Harbor pins
And their blue-eyed
Gray-haired Catholic
Union nurses handing out
Photocopied flyers of what
It means to be American

You fell in love
With a platform beauty
On a brewery tabletop
Her arms raised
Above her head in
Celebration of
Her youth

You watched her as she
Rallied would-be troops
To the beer-inflected cause
Of all-night joy
And walked her home
Come early morning
With your coat draped across
Her shoulders

University of San Francisco

The sisters of mercy still sleep on the lawn
They say prayers in their sleep, they turn like the wind

You want to make love to each of their dreams
You want to tell them the church of their bodies
Is where faith begins

Grace

There was no way you could have
Known she would be there,
Summer in the autumn grass,
Sound within a silent film.

But when she showed you
How to carve the moon from sky
Like rumor from a tongue,

You lay down beneath her in the darkness
And told her where it was you hurt.

Soon Enough

And in time such echoes lose the force of their convictions
The violence that was once the sound of cities burning
Becomes the ghost whose howling young lovers can ignore

Watch as you weave like a drunken man between the trees
Your vengeance rustling
Only the fallen leaves of autumn's past

A Winter's Tale

The boys in harbor coats that sit upon the boardwalk
Watch the angels giggle at their reflections in a frozen sea

All the young Hermiones carve their initials into salt
And snowflakes thread themselves into hair and onto wings
The gaze of a dreaming nation knows no season

Laguna Rainmaker

Carrying rain like a postcard
Stamped with the autumn of your desires
The photograph of a castle reminding you
Of a children's book that used
To help you sleep as a child on its colored cover

You place it into the mailbox
Of the girl that you love
Hoping to prove to her
That you can deliver the weather that she loves
For as long as the two of you shall live

Fountain Intermezzo

Children play in the fountain
In front of the San Diego Museum of Art

They splash their mothers and fathers
They try to do handstands in the tiled shallows
They squeeze out every minute of summer joy
Their parents aware they will see no paintings more lovely
Than what they are watching outside

Matisse's *Pastorale*, 1905

This is a picnic in the years before the wars were fought,
See the colors, the blues and greens,
The motion of the trees,
The piper playing odes
To the child that has emerged from sleep.

And these gardens that the nudes would keep,
Their bodies certain
Of the eternal pageant that the sun would seek,
A farmer bringing
Food to an Eden by the sea,
The skyline dappled like the coats of bees,
And the red-haired girl,
Sitting with the patience of a Helen long set free.

Matisse's View of Notre Dame, 1914

The face of the church has windows for eyes,
A green dimple for Eden,
A whirlwind of brushstrokes
That run out of breath at the lower edges of canvas,
The palette of a sprinter
Who never saved enough for his run home.

Are those clouds trying to slip through the stained glass
Of guilt and commandments?
Is that the head of a swan
Swimming towards Eve in the west?

The scholars say this was the apex of your dance
With abstraction,
A quest for divinity within the mazes of space and geometry,
But all you know is that the blue you employ
Is the color of a sky aware of its good fortune
To model for genius,
The chapel façade a landscape for dreaming and love.

Wild Garden

The sorrow of olives after the sun has descended,
Like a tired king trudging down steps to the sea,
Leaving behind the ramparts and turrets
He has constructed for the sake of his city,
He has forgotten the words to the prayers he was taught.

He would paint this portrait if his visibility were better,
But all he can see from here
Is the silhouette of the damned,
The shadow of love that trails him like a ghost.

An Early Tribe

The mute Scheherazades
Make their way through the forests of light.

They lick the shells of turtles for luck,
They rub the petals of flowers
Against their elbows for warmth.

Their narratives are like the clocks in the trees,
Slow hands ticking into love
As the leaves turn green, then red, then brown.

The fall lasts for many nights,
The apples have replaced the stars,
The painters have all left for ridges that reside closer to sky.

I wish you could hear them,
Mingling breath into courage,
Starving their captors by spilling their nourishments
Onto stones, into rivers,
Across the marrow of seasons that the grass represents.

Their tales of love and forgiveness,
Their tales of sorrow and force,
Their visions of children with two hearts
And fathers who rise from the seas,
Script themselves for this journey's heritage,
Birthing the many lives they require.

A Psalm

The dress of all azaleas
The north of broken compass
The pageant of twelve saxophones
The gold of summer's photograph

We lean our yesterdays against kaleidoscope
We diagram our treasure maps within our palms
What rust becomes inside all shorelines
We tend with kerchiefs made of cloud and sun

The Thief and His Father

The thief speaks to his father by telephone,
Each day at the same time, the only constant
In a life shaped by foreign beds, meals taken
At makeshift tables, friendships abandoned
In the interests of sovereignty.

The father worries that his son, the thief,
Who has always been a thief, who once
Presented the father with a stained glass
Window he had stolen from the shrine
At a local church, has yet to find love,
Which is the only way the father believes
That the son, who enjoys these conversations
With his father, will ever change.

The son, who will always be a thief,
Does not know how to tell his father
That he finds love every day, that he
Falls into love more often than he steals.
It is all he has stolen for years, actually,
It is all he has stolen since the church
Window, in truth, the window that etched
The silent beauty of angels into his dreams,
The angels he watches pass in the streets
Beyond the phone booth from where he stands,
Speaking to his father, who does not know,
And will never know, the nature of his son's thievery.

The Orpheus Songs

Morning like an infected swan,
Whiteness commensurate with everything lost,
A canvas where once was palette.

I no longer trust my instincts.
I hesitate on subway platforms,
I check the locks too many times,
I wade into seas I once dove beneath.

The heritage of another country,
Where ghosts island hop
With the ease of children skipping rope,
Is no Avalon,
And this chorus of glass must fear its own octave—
Lorries for voices,
Disease the boldest Narcissus,
The petals in the grove bloodied upon my return.

Thieves were but the gospels awakened,
They mistook scepters for globes,
Blunting a world whose love they could not conceive.
Though the stars dismount at your crossing,
I'll never lift my eyes again.